Friends and Followers

by
Sheryl Herbert

Illustrated by Simon

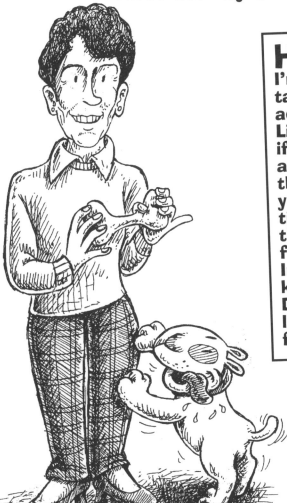

Hello there!
I'm Sheryl and I'm taking you on another adventure with the Livewires. Don't worry if you haven't been on an adventure with them before—I know you'll have a great time getting to know them and learning a few things too. I have! In case you don't know who everyone is Digit has written you a letter, so get ready for some action!

Text copyright © Sheryl Herbert 1997

Illustrations copyright © Simon Smith 1997

The author asserts the moral right to
be identified as the author of this work

Published by
The Bible Reading Fellowship
Peter's Way, Sandy Lane West
Oxford OX4 5HG
ISBN 0 7459 3522 2
Albatross Books Pty Ltd
PO Box 320, Sutherland
NSW 2232, Australia
ISBN 0 7324 1564 0

First edition 1997

10 9 8 7 6 5 4 3 2 1 0

Acknowledgments
Unless otherwise stated, scripture quotations are
taken from the Good News Bible published by The
Bible Societies/HarperCollins Publishers Ltd UK ©
American Bible Society, 1966, 1971, 1976, 1992

A catalogue record for this book is
available from the British Library

Printed and bound in Malta
by Interprint Limited

**An imprint of
The Bible Reading
Fellowship**

Hi! I'm Digit and I've just thrown that spectacular paper plane across the room. It's heading for my twin sister, Quartz, who's on the top bunk. She looks as if she's helping out in the game of cards. Wonder who's winning? I'm surprised Tim can see the cards through that hair of his, and Data looks happy—so I think it must be her. Now I think I'll just get Annie-log to stop doing her homework—after all it looks as if Little Ben's finished reading a story to Tempo. Well, dogs can't read by themselves, can they?!

Rain, rain, rain—that's all it seems to have done this holiday. Tim's been complaining it's too wet even for football, and Quartz has been a pain 'cos she hasn't been to a party or a disco for ages. Annie-log's quite happy though—she's got a new computer game—'Follow the Leader'. You have to decide on a leader and follow the instructions. Well, she was playing it when suddenly without any warning Boot's screen started flashing. When it stopped, we looked in amazement. It said, 'An invitation to find out about some of the greatest leaders'. There was a whirring sound and before we knew what was happening Boot had whisked us up into the air and into his disk drive. Whooaa... here we go!

Where are we now Annie-log?

I'm not sure. It's rather empty apart from those sheep over there.

Hey this is a great place for football. We could hold the Cup Final here. Ugh! Mind those sheep droppings though!

Well Boot, where have we landed up this time?

One day when Moses was taking care of the sheep and goats of his father-in-law Jethro, the priest of Midian, he led the flock across the desert and came to Sinai, the holy mountain.

EXODUS 3:1

This is a lonely place isn't it? Only sheep and goats for company.

?

Look! There's a man over there. I wonder if he is Moses.

Do you think he'll hear us if we shout?

Don't be silly—we'd frighten the sheep! You know what sheep are like—the slightest sound and off they go. They can't be used to much noise in this place.

Hey—look over there—something is happening!

The Livewires turned to see what had caught Little Ben's attention. Have you any idea what it could be?

The Livewires were so surprised by what they saw that they decided to watch from behind a rock. As they peered around the rock they could see the strangest sight—a bush was on fire and Moses was going up to it. They watch, open-eyed in amazement.

Wow! look at those shapes and colours! Terrific! Wish I'd brought my camera.

He's going towards the bush, and look, he's taking his shoes off!

That's strange—the bush isn't burning up even though it's on fire. It's weird.

Let's go closer. I'm sure I can hear someone talking to him, but I can't see anyone.

When the Lord saw that Moses was coming closer, he called to him from the middle of the bush and said, 'Moses! Moses!'

That was God's voice.

EXODUS 3:4

The Livewires turned to look at Tychi in amazement. 'God?' said Digit, 'He must be pretty important for God to know his name and to talk to him.' 'Well,' said Annie-log, 'he doesn't look too important—he's only a shepherd.'

Hmmm—I thought we were all important—more important, where's my bone? I hope I didn't leave it behind.

We are all important to God. He knows each one of us by name.

Moses Moses

Dear God, you know each one of us by name because...

we are all special and important to you. Amen

You could colour in the picture of the brightly burning bush and write what the Livewires heard in the speech bubble. Why is it that God knows each one of us by name? Write your answer in this cloud:

5

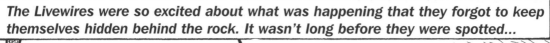
The Livewires were so excited about what was happening that they forgot to keep themselves hidden behind the rock. It wasn't long before they were spotted...

Hello! Where did you lot spring from?

Well, we sort of landed... We're the Livewires and this is our computer, Boot.

Now I am sending you to the King of Egypt so that you can lead my people out of his country.

EXODUS 3:10

Gosh! Your funny Boot seems to know what God said to me!

You mean God wants you to do that? That's a BIG job. Why are the Israelites in Egypt anyway?

Moses sighed. 'It all started a long time ago, he said, 'when Joseph, who was an Israelite, was sold to the Egyptians. He became an important person in Egypt. Then there was a famine and Joseph's family came to Egypt looking for food—it's all part of another adventure. Anyway it turned out that Joseph's family—who were all Israelites—went to live in Egypt with Joseph. They were treated well in Egypt until this new king came along.

Data didn't like to think of people being treated badly—it reminded her of the time she was bullied at school. She wanted to know what Moses was going to do.

Why doesn't this new king treat them nicely?

I expect he's afraid because the Israelites are growing in number. But that's no excuse for being cruel to them.

I don't know. I'm nobody special—how can I go to the king and bring the Israelites out of Egypt?

Dear God, please help me to make the right choice when there's something you want me to do. Amen.

Poor Moses—he is being asked to do a big job. Do you think he'll say yes or no?

☑ YES   ❏ NO

Tick the box and then think about how you feel when you are asked to do something difficult. Perhaps you could say this prayer.

Moses sat with the Livewires on the rock and stared at the burning bush. He had to make a decision and he felt very alone. Then God spoke to him again...

Suddenly they all felt happier and jumped up to join Tim playing football. He kicked the ball to Moses who kicked it back.

Moses didn't answer. He was deep in thought.

Moses was being asked to do something which was very hard. You can probably think of times when you have had to do something difficult. Tick the box if you have had to do any of the following:

- ☑ *Own up to not telling the truth*
- ☑ *Admit you broke something*
- ☑ *Say sorry to someone*
- ☑ *Forgive someone who has been unkind to you*
- ☑ *Struggle with very hard work at school*

If you haven't had to do any of these, perhaps you can think of another difficult thing you've done...

Thank you God for helping me when I have something difficult to do.

The Livewires could see that Moses had a problem.

I don't think the Israelites will believe that God appeared to me. How will I explain all this to them and to the Egyptians?

So the Lord asked him, 'What are you holding?'

EXODUS 4:2

A stick!

Moses threw the stick he was holding to the ground and it became a snake. He picked it up by its tail and it became a stick again!

Yipes! A snake! Now if that had been a rabbit...!

Moses then put his hand into his robe and when he brought it out it was covered in white spots.

Oh! Your hand looks like snow!

Moses put his hand back inside his robe and when he took it out this time it was healthy again.

That's quite something!

Yes, they're signs that God has given me to show the people if they don't believe me.

Watch out, there's another snake! Oh, sorry, it's only a piece of rope... I didn't mean to frighten you all!

The Livewires were very impressed with the signs that God had given to Moses. They were sure he would be able to convince both the Israelites and the Egyptians now. And Moses told them that God had given him a third sign—if the people still didn't believe him then he was to take some water from the River Nile and God would make it turn into blood.

He doesn't look very happy about it.

He's bound to do it now.

He still seems a bit afraid.

Of course he'll do it!

I'm not so sure.

I don't know...

Well, if I'd thrown my rope down and it had turned into a snake I would jolly well have been convinced. You've only got to follow God's orders, Moses!

Sometimes that's easier said than done—especially when you feel on your own.

Moses has a brother, Aaron...

God said... 'I will help you both to speak, and I will tell you both what to do. Aaron will be your spokesman and speak to the people for you.'

EXODUS 4:15–16

At last! Now Moses doesn't have to feel that he's doing a hard job all on his own.

This wordsearch has words which belong in the story of how God called Moses to rescue his people from the Egyptians. As you find the words, can you remember how they fit into the story?

ISRAELITES SINAI AARON DESERT SHEEP SNAKE EGYPT KING GOATS MOSES

E P S H E E P G A B
G N I K S E S O M F
Y S N A K E D A C I
P A A R O N L T O G
T S I U T R E S E D
I S R A E L I T E S

9

Sunday
Look ahead to the coming week. Think of someone you know who may feel lonely, and think of a way to help them.

Monday
Think about something you have to do this week. Ask God to help you.

Tuesday
Do you think Moses should go to the King of Egypt? Why?

Wednesday
Find a smooth pebble and write your name on it. Put it somewhere in your bedroom to remind yourself that God knows your name and loves you.

Thursday
Remember all those people who love you. Perhaps you could draw a picture of some of them?

Friday

Dear God, please help all those children who are alone to have one friend they can talk to. Help me when I feel lonely to know that you are with me.

Saturday
Write down something nice that has happened today.

Come on Annie-log, let's move out of here and find some action. It's too quiet in the desert for me.

So Annie-log started to type 'EXIT' onto Boot's keyboard. But she got no further than EX... when Boot began to whirr and they found themselves being whooshed into his disk drive in a cloud of hot sand...

Oh no! We're still in the desert! Annie-log, I asked you to get us out of here...

Well I typed in EX and he whooshed before I could type in IT! Look, there's Moses again. Who is that with him? Hi, Moses... It's us again!

Thought you lot had gone for good. This is my brother Aaron—These are the Livewires. They seem to pop up all over the place—thanks to Boot.

Have you told Aaron about the burning bush?

Yes, I have, and guess what? Aaron has agreed to come along and help me—just as God suggested! We're on our way to Egypt. Coming?

You bet! We don't want to miss out on the action!

So off they all went to Egypt, Tim kicking his football, Data skipping with her rope and Tempo sniffing for rabbits as they went. Moses gathered the Israelite leaders together and told them what had happened. He performed the miracles God had given him in front of the people.

They believed, and when they heard how the Lord had come to them and had seen how they were being treated cruelly, they bowed down and worshipped.

EXODUS 4:31

I'm glad Aaron has come to help Moses. Friends can really help us, particularly when we have something hard to do.

Yes, and don't the Israel-ites look pleased to know that God hasn't forgotten them? What's the next step then, Moses?

We've got to go to the king. Come on, let's not waste time!

Thank you God that you never forget us.

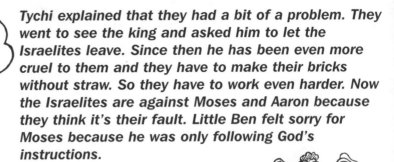

Moses and Aaron look a bit miserable. I wonder what's wrong?

Tychi explained that they had a bit of a problem. They went to see the king and asked him to let the Israelites leave. Since then he has been even more cruel to them and they have to make their bricks without straw. So they have to work even harder. Now the Israelites are against Moses and Aaron because they think it's their fault. Little Ben felt sorry for Moses because he was only following God's instructions.

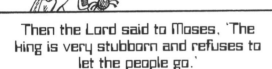

Then the Lord said to Moses, 'The king is very stubborn and refuses to let the people go.'

EXODUS 7:14

Stubborn? That's what Tim called me when I wouldn't chase the ball. Wonder what it means?

The Livewires wondered about the meaning of stubborn. Annie-log suggested that if someone was stubborn they would stick by something even if they knew they were in the wrong. They wouldn't change their mind. Little Ben was worried that the king wouldn't change HIS mind and let the Israelites go. Moses said, 'I think it might take some time. We'll have to wait and see.'

Come on... a game of football will take our mind off things.

Write down a time when you have been stubborn about something. You may like to say sorry to God for that time. Here is a prayer to help you:

Matthew being horbble

Dear God, I am sorry when I refused to...
do things what other people want me to do
please forgive me.

The Livewires went off to explore. They noticed some very strange things happening and decided to go back to Moses to see if he knew what was going on.

It's not very nice around here is it? Look at those poor animals—all dead. Tempo, come away. Let me put this rope around you.

I'm glad I'm not an Egyptian dog. I might be dead by now!

Data asked Moses what was happening and why all the animals were dead. She told him they had seen some strange things. Moses said, 'The king of Egypt still won't let the Israelites go, so God is having to punish the Egyptians to make the king change his mind.'

First of all we saw all the water in Egypt turned to blood and then there were frogs everywhere!

Yes! These are called the plagues.

The next one was all the gnats. They were everywhere! Digit and Tempo both complained that they had been bitten!

Then there were all those flies! They were buzzing around everywhere.

Trouble is, even after the water changing to blood, the frogs, the gnats and the flies, the king still wouldn't let the Israelites go. And now all the animals are dead.

He really is stubborn.

The king asked what had happened and was told that none of the animals of the Israelites had died. But he was stubborn and would not let the people go.

EXODUS 9:7

Divide a piece of paper into 10 squares. Draw cartoon pictures of the first five plagues in the first five squares.

Then the Lord said to Moses and Aaron, 'Take a few handfuls of ashes from a furnace; Moses shall throw them into the air in front of the king.'

EXODUS 9:8

Ugh! Look! All the Egyptians are covered in horrible boils. Is this another plague to try to make the king change his mind?

Ouch! What was that? It looks like hail, but it's bigger than any hail I've ever seen. Is this another plague? I wish the king would hurry up and let the Israelites go!

Moses reminded them that the king was a stubborn man. He didn't want to lose all his slaves. Following the boils and the hail, Egypt was overrun by locusts, which are like huge grasshoppers. These ate all the crops. After this Egypt was in total darkness. Nobody could see anything at all.

Moses, do you think you'll ever lead the Israelites out of Egypt?

I'm sure I will. Hang around a bit longer.

Did I miss the locusts? Bet they would have been tasty!

Continue drawing your strip cartoon of the plagues. Draw the next 4 plagues, boils, hail, locusts and darkness, in the next 4 boxes.

You must celebrate this day as a religious festival to remind you of what I, the Lord, have done. Celebrate it for all time to come.

What has happened that is important enough to be remembered every year?

Why is everyone in Egypt looking so sad?

EXODUS 12:14

Moses told them it was now the time to leave Egypt. The first-born of all the Egyptians had died, so at last the king had agreed to let the Israelites go. Little Ben thought it was a shame the king was so stubborn that he wouldn't agree until something as sad as this happened. Little Ben wondered what had happened to the Israelites.

They were to kill a lamb and smear some of the blood on their doorposts, then prepare a meal with the meat and bitter herbs and bake unleavened bread, which was quick to prepare.

This was the sign God gave them so that the angel of death would know to pass over them. This is what God has told them to remember every year—the Passover.

Got it! Passover! Pass over them. Always wondered what it meant!

God doesn't want the Israelites ever to forget how he led them out of slavery. Come on then, let's get started before the king changes his mind.

He wouldn't! ...Would he?!!!!

Thank you Father God for leading the people of Israel out of Egypt.

Complete your strip cartoon by drawing a picture of the Passover meal in square 10.

There's loads and loads of them. I didn't realize there were quite so many Israelites in Egypt!

We'd better stick close together or we'll get lost in this crowd.

This is brilliant. Everyone seems so happy.

All we need is some music and we could have a party. Look! They're singing and dancing down there. I'm going to join them.

Quartz told the others she wouldn't get lost. When they stopped Tim went to see what was happening as they all seemed to be moaning about Moses. He asked if they had come the wrong way.

The Red Sea was in front of the Israelites and some of them had seen the Egyptian army in the distance, coming after them.

It's OK God's not worried. Listen...

Don't be afraid! Stand your ground, and you will see what the Lord will do to save you today; you will never see these Egyptians again.

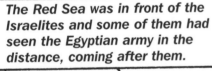

EXODUS 14:13

Thank you God that you are so powerful.

Look! Moses is raising his stick and the sea is parting. What a sight! Off we go! Hold onto the rope everyone!

Lovely smells. Bliss...

Data said they should have known God wouldn't let them down after all the trouble he went to to get them out of Egypt.

He is a pretty powerful God!

Moses and the Israelites were able to cross the Red Sea safely. As soon as they were across, the sea returned, covering all the Egyptians who were following them.

Sunday
Remember to thank God for your food, and ask him to help those people who do not have enough to eat.

Monday
The Israelites moaned to Moses as soon as they thought something was wrong. Do you ever moan about things? Write down something you have moaned about and say sorry to God for moaning!

Tuesday
What were the first four plagues?

Wednesday
What were the next four plagues?

Thursday
Can you remember the last two plagues? What does Passover mean?

Friday
If you have a friend who is not well, make a little 'Get Well' card to give—or you could make a 'Thank You' card for someone who has helped you.

Saturday
Moses needed courage to do what God wanted him to do. There may be something you need courage to do. Why not write it down and ask God to help you?

Now, come on Boot, I'm fed up with all this sand. How about moving us on?

In her hurry Annie-log pressed the wrong key. Once again there was a whirr and a whoosh and a lot of hot sand started blowing around them...

The Livewires didn't think Boot was being very helpful—and they didn't know what it meant to be tempted by the devil. Digit got out his sketch pad and started to doodle a puzzle.

Digit has written this sentence about being tempted, but he has missed out all the vowels: a, e, i, o, u. Can you work out what he is saying?

To tempt someone means to try to get them to do something they shouldn't do

The Livewires sat quietly waiting to see if anything was going to happen. It all seemed so quiet.

Anybody got any chocolate left? I'm starving.

Me too! It's ages since we last ate.

It's all right for you, Boot. You don't need food and drink to keep you going.

Just microchips!

After spending forty days and nights without food, Jesus was hungry.

MATTHEW 4:2

You mean this is the desert where Jesus spent forty days and nights? And he didn't have anything to eat? He must have been mega starving!!

And we've been complaining because we haven't eaten for a couple of hours.

The Livewires sat quietly for some time thinking about what it must be like to be really, really hungry. Even Tim stopped playing with his football. They thought about some of the sad pictures they had seen on television of children who were starving.

At least we know we'll soon have something to eat. Some children in the world are always hungry, and they can't do anything about it.

Thank you God that I have enough food to eat every day. Please help all those children who are starving. I pray for all those who are trying to help them.

Can you think of ways to help people who haven't got enough food?

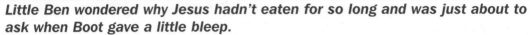

Little Ben wondered why Jesus hadn't eaten for so long and was just about to ask when Boot gave a little bleep.

Then the Devil came to him and said, 'If you are God's Son, order these stones to turn into bread.'

MATTHEW 4:3

Goodness! Do you mean to say that the devil suggested that Jesus should turn the stones into bread?

Well after all he must have been pretty hungry—and if he is God's Son he surely would have been able to do it, wouldn't he?

Tychi gave a little tut. She thought the Livewires must have got a little confused and forgotten Boot's message earlier on. Do you remember it? Perhaps you can work it out from Tychi's clue?

.devil the by tempted be to desert the into Jesus led Spirit the Then

But I'm still not sure what it means to be tempted. What was that doodle you were doing earlier, Digit?

Dear God, help us to know the right thing to do and then give us the courage to do it.

To tempt someone means to try to get them to do something they shouldn't do.

Tim still couldn't understand why Jesus shouldn't turn the stones into bread, so Tychi explained that it would have been wrong for Jesus to do as the devil suggested because he would have been obeying him and not God.

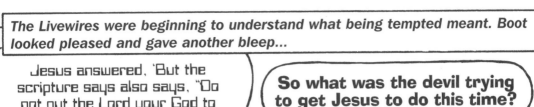

The Livewires were beginning to understand what being tempted meant. Boot looked pleased and gave another bleep...

Jesus answered, 'But the scripture says also says, "Do not put the Lord your God to the test."'

MATTHEW 4:7

So what was the devil trying to get Jesus to do this time?

Jesus was being tempted to jump from the top of the temple in Jerusalem.

Jesus must have been getting pretty tired. It would have been easy to give in and do something the devil suggested just to get rid of him. I know I've done that before.

Hope this doesn't go on for too long—I want to play football!

Just be quiet Tim and stop moaning. I want to know what happened next. I mean, how much longer can Jesus keep saying 'No'? Like Data, I find it very hard to keep saying no if someone keeps on at me.

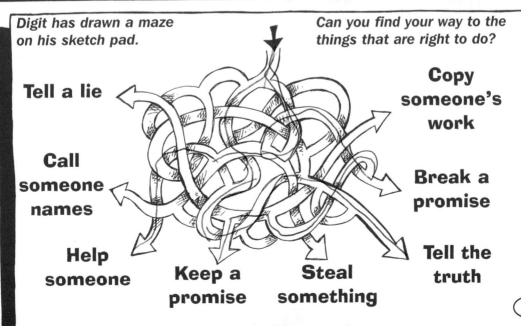

Digit has drawn a maze on his sketch pad.

Can you find your way to the things that are right to do?

Tell a lie

Copy someone's work

Call someone names

Break a promise

Help someone

Keep a promise

Steal something

Tell the truth

The Livewires chatted about times they had been tempted to do something they knew they shouldn't do. They agreed how hard it was to keep saying no to someone. Apart from Tim, they all wanted to see what Boot would tell them next.

> **Anybody for football ?**

> **NO!!!**

> Then the Devil took Jesus to a very high mountain and showed him all the kingdoms of the world in all their greatness. 'All this I will give you,' the Devil said, 'if you kneel down and worship me.'

> MATTHEW 4:8-9

The Livewires held their breath, hardly daring to think about such a temptation, and wondered what Jesus had said.

> MATTHEW 4:10

> Then Jesus answered, 'Go away, Satan! The scripture says, "Worship the Lord your God and serve only him!" '

The Livewires let out a sigh of relief when they heard Jesus' answer. They suddenly realized how much courage it can take to do the right thing.

Can you remember what the three things were that the devil used to tempt Jesus? Draw a picture of them and write Jesus' reply underneath your picture.

> **I am glad Jesus didn't give in. I'm going to ask for courage next time I'm tempted to do something which I shouldn't!**

Then the Devil left Jesus; and angels came helped him.

MATTHEW 4:11

Wow! Angels! I bet Jesus was pleased to see them.

The Livewires decided to draw a picture of the angels helping Jesus. Perhaps you'd like to help them by colouring it in?

Even Tim sat quietly and joined in, until he suddenly jumped up and said...

Right! Let's...

TIM!!!!

Actually, I was going to say let's remember what Jesus said to the devil. The next time I'm tempted to play football instead of going to church, I'll remember Jesus and say 'No!'

Yeah, and the next time I'm tempted to play on my computer instead of doing my homework, I'll say 'No!' Come on, let's have a game of football.

I'll use the rope for a goal.

While the Livewires are playing their game, perhaps you could see how many different words you can make using the letters in the word TEMPTATION.

Sunday
Take time to enjoy a day with family and friends.

Monday
Try to remember to say a special thank you to someone today.

Tuesday
I will try to say 'no' when I am tempted to...

Wednesday
Angels came and helped Jesus after his difficult time. Who do you think needs your help?

Thursday
Draw a picture of what you think the desert where Jesus was tempted looked like.

Friday

> **Thank you God that when I am tempted to do something I shouldn't, you can help me to say 'No!'**

Saturday
Think of one thing you can do today to help someone.

6 – 0

Please Boot, GET US OUT OF THE DESERT!!!!

Boot bleeped and soon they were on their way...

Oh, no! I don't believe it— more sand!! BOOT! ...

But as Quartz looked around her she saw they were at the edge of a bright, sparkling blue sea. She said sorry to Boot for shouting at him and decided to paddle her toes in the water. The rest of the Livewires decided to do the same. It was so refreshing. They had a lovely time splashing each other. Boot decided it was safer to sit on the edge and watch.

This is Lake Galilee where Jesus first met Simon Peter and Andrew. They used to be fishermen.

Simon Peter and Andrew were two of the first followers of Jesus.

As Jesus walked along the shore of Lake Galilee, he saw two fishermen Simon (called Peter) and his brother Andrew, catching fish in the lake with a net. Jesus said to them, 'Come with me, and I will teach you to catch people.'

MATTHEW 4:18-19

I wonder what it was like following Jesus? Do you think we'll meet some of the people who followed him?

The Livewires started talking about the sort of leader Jesus was and why people followed him. In the sand they drew an outline of a person, like this...

Annie-log thought Jesus would have been kind so she wrote the word 'kind' inside the outline. Can you think of any words to describe Jesus? If you can, write them in the outline. You may be able to add others as you follow the Livewires through this adventure.

As the Livewires looked around, they saw two fishermen. They thought they would ask them if they knew anything about the followers of Jesus. Little Ben decided to try and catch some fish using Data's rope as a fishing line.

Mmm... fresh fish... lovely.

Fish? Lots of bones!!

As they were waiting for the fish to bite, the fishermen came up and started chatting to them. The Livewires asked them if they knew any of the people who followed Jesus.

Why of course—we are his followers— he's a great leader. Meet my brother Simon, and two friends, James and John. They're brothers too.

Were you all followers of Jesus? Did you have to be specially trained or clever, or anything like that?

Andrew explained that they had been ordinary fishermen when Jesus came along and called them to follow him. From that time their lives had changed, even though they were only fishermen, he still wanted them to follow him. Jesus seemed so kind and caring that they left their jobs as fishermen and followed him.

Can you see who has caught the fish?

You've caught a fish!!

Sure enough, the Livewires pulled in the slippery fish. The fishermen showed them how to cook it, and they ate it with their new friends, who were eager to tell them stories of Jesus.

Can you find another word on this page which describes Jesus? Write it in the outline of the person.

The Livewires were enjoying listening to Simon and Andrew tell them stories about Jesus.

Who else followed Jesus?

Jesus left that place, and as he walked along, he saw a tax collector, named Matthew, sitting in his office. He said to him, 'Follow me.'

MATTHEW 9:9

Simon and Andrew took the Livewires along to meet their friend. Matthew said that Jesus was different from all the other leaders that he had known because he didn't always do what people expected him to do.

What do you mean?

As a tax-collector I worked for the Romans, who were our enemies. Not only that, we cheated ordinary people and became rich. We were hated by our own people. But Jesus still asked me to follow him. Some other leaders thought he was making a big mistake.

I see—so what happened to make you follow him?

When Jesus asked me to follow him I just couldn't say no. No one else had shown they wanted me or cared for me before. So I went...

Did you continue to follow Jesus?

Oh yes. He loved me and accepted me, even though I had been doing wrong. He showed me how to put things right.

From the last couple of pages think of a few other words to describe Jesus that you could put into the outline.

Matthew, Simon and Andrew continued to talk to the Livewires about Jesus. The Livewires wanted to know what sort of things Jesus had done when he was with them. Before any of them had a chance to answer this question, Boot jumped up and down, bleeping excitedly.

Jesus went round visiting all the towns and villages. He taught in the synagogues, preached the Good News about the Kingdom, and healed people with every kind of disease and sickness.

Hey! Your friend is right—that's what Jesus did. We all helped him do those things too. Jesus was a very good teacher and helped us to understand things that were quite hard. He also made some people better when they were ill. Jesus had important things to say to people so he needed people like us to follow him and help him tell others about God.

MATTHEW 9.35

Thank you, dear Lord that you welcome us when we come to you. Amen.

Matthew went on to say that so many people followed Jesus because he helped them understand things and he cared for them, sometimes when nobody else did. He welcomed everybody who wanted to follow him.

The Livewires have thought of some more words to go into the outline. Have you? They have thought of: teacher, preacher, welcoming. Can you think of some different ones?

After some time, Data suddenly chirped up that she hadn't heard them mention any women who were followers of Jesus, and she wondered if there were any.

As soon as she said this, Boot gave a little bleep, and they found themselves being taken down a dusty path, passing a few houses on the way. Boot landed them outside a small house at the end of the path. It was Mary's house and Simon introduced Mary to the Livewires.

All those we've spoken to so far have been men—we wanted to meet a woman.

Well, I'm pleased to meet you! Yes, I followed Jesus, even though I am a woman!

So?! What has being a woman got to do with it?

Around here, women are not thought of as being important. They aren't listened to—but it didn't make any difference to Jesus. Jesus accepted men and women, and treated each one kindly.

Quartz asked Mary if that was why she had followed Jesus. Mary said it was one of the reasons, but he had also made her feel special, and loved.

Nobody loved me before Jesus. I had done things wrong so no one wanted to talk to me or be friends with me. Jesus forgave me and helped me to live a better life.

Mary then told them that something very special had happened after Jesus had died. She had gone to the visit his tomb and she was the first person to actually see Jesus alive again.

At first I thought he was the gardener, but when I spoke to him, he replied...

...'Mary!' She turned towards him and said in Hebrew, 'Rabboni!' (This means 'Teacher.')

Oh yes! That's right!

JOHN 20:16

Thank you Jesus for calling people to follow you.

Can you think of another word to go into the outline?

As they sat listening to different people the Livewires realized that all the followers of Jesus were different.

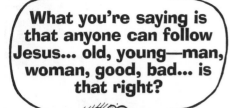

What you're saying is that anyone can follow Jesus... old, young—man, woman, good, bad... is that right?

Yes, you've got it! Anyone...

Even children?

Jesus said, 'Let the children come to me and do not stop them, because the Kingdom of heaven belongs to such as these.'

MATTHEW 19.14

That's brilliant!!

Write your name on the invitation and colour it in:

Dear Johanna.
You are invited to follow me
lots of love from Jesus

Thank you Jesus that I can follow you.

Have you been able to add any more words to describe Jesus? Did you think of any of these words? kind loving strong forgiving accepting special

Sunday
Draw a picture of a leader you know. It might be a Cub leader, Brownie leader, teacher or church leader.

Monday
Write what you like about the leader you have drawn.

Tuesday
Here is a prayer for your leader:

> **Dear God please help... in all the work she/he does. Please look after her/him and keep her/him safe.**

Wednesday
Some of Jesus' followers were fishermen. Can you remember their names?

Thursday
How do you think Matthew felt when Jesus called him?

Friday
Draw a picture of Matthew.

Saturday
Design your own invitation card to follow Jesus.

The Livewires were unusually quiet. No one was speaking, faces were glum. It was a sad place to be. Can you guess why? There had been lots of silly quarrels, and now they were not speaking to each other. They had said horrible things to each other and about each other, they wouldn't share with each other and now no one was going to be the first to put things right. It went on like this for some time.

After a while Tychi and Boot decided they could not stand the silence any longer and took things into their own hands. They decided the Livewires needed a bit of help to sort out their friendships.

Before anyone knew what was happening there was a whirr and a whoosh and the Livewires found themselves standing outside a strange building.

Excuse me for asking, but what's going on? Where are we?

Friends... Boot and I could not stand things any longer, so we are taking you on a tour to find out about being friends. We're going to start outside the temple built by Solomon—a very wise king. He had lots of wise things to say about friends.

The Livewires didn't say anything but just looked at each other—thinking about things they had said about each other.

Gossip is spread by wicked people; they stir up trouble and break up friendships.

PROVERBS 16:28

What do you think the Livewires are thinking? Fill in their thought bubbles.

shall I say sorry

I feel really bad now

I cant belive its ended up like this

Sposs, I should say sorry to Annie—

Right, Boot, off we go! Next stop coming up.

The Livewires found themselves sitting on a hillside with a large group of people. They were all talking about how Jesus had told them a story in answer to a question Peter had asked about how often he should forgive his brother.

'No, not seven times,' answered Jesus, 'but seventy times seven.'

MATTHEW 18:22

The story Jesus had told was about a master who forgave his servant for owing him lots of money. The servant went out and would not forgive another servant for owing him a small amount of money. The master heard about this and was angry. He sent the servant to jail because he would not forgive the man for owing him a little amount.

The Livewires looked at each other, then quietly began to say sorry and asked to be forgiven.

I'm sorry for ignoring you.

Sorry I ruined your game.

Sorry I wouldn't play.

Sorry I wouldn't lend you my CD.

Sorry I let you down.

I'm sorry I called you names.

Sorry I hid the ball!!

Tychi and Boot looked pleased with themselves.

Right then, Boot, mission accomplished— they're at least talking to one another now. Where to next?

Are we all forgiven? YES!!!

Dear God, I am sorry...

that I've sometimes forgotten the most important things of life. Amen

Boot had a bright idea and began typing on his own keyboard...

Perhaps you would like to say sorry for something? Write it in the cloud...

The Livewires looked around—no temple here—only fields and bushes. They saw a young man, who turned towards them, looking very frightened. He asked them if they were from Saul's army, coming to kill him.

Of course not! We're the Livewires, on an adventure trail to find out about friendship.

We've been having a few quarrels and Tychi and Boot decided we needed a bit of help. So here we are. Who are you?

My name's David and I can give you a very good tip about being friends. Be loyal to your friends, even when things get difficult.

Why are you here on your own, afraid someone is going to kill you?

King Saul is very jealous of me and wants to kill me. But his son, Jonathan, is my best friend. He wants to please his dad, but he has promised to be loyal to me, so he is helping me to escape from the King.

Jonathan said, 'May our promise to each other be unbroken.'

We must remember that.

How about a quick game of football before we go?

1 SAMUEL 20:16

David, forgetting about King Saul for a while, enjoyed a game with the Livewires.

This is going pretty well, Boot—next stop coming up...

Dear God, thank you for my friends. Megs Los Clot Emma even though sometimes I and them fell left out Amen

34

Have you ever stuck by someone, even though things were very hard? Write your friend's name in the cloud.

Once again the Livewires found themselves with a crowd of people. They were standing outside a small house.

Look at that house. It's got an outside staircase leading up to a flat roof.

Round the corner came four men, carrying a friend who couldn't walk. They struggled to get through the crowd.

Look! They're going up onto the roof. Let's follow!

The Livewires arrived on the roof just in time to see the men making a hole in the roof and slowly letting their friend through it. The Livewires peered down the hole.

Look, there's Jesus down there!

'I tell you, get up, pick up your mat and go home.'

MARK 2:11

The Livewires watched in amazement as the man walked away. They dashed down the stairs and ran after him, wanting to know more.

Er... excuse me, but we saw what happened back there. Did you know Jesus would heal you?

Oh, yes, I've heard so much about him! It's all thanks to my good friends who carried me to Jesus. And look... I can walk, run, jump... all because my friends cared enough.

My friend Tim takes me for walks.

Another successful mission, Boot. Onward we go!

Dear Jesus, help me to care for my friends and help them whenever I can.

Why not colour in this page?

And onward they went, with Boot and Tychi leading the way. Soon they heard music and laughter—Quartz's ears pricked up.

Quickly, there's a party... let's see if we can join in. Perhaps it's somebody's birthday. Come on you lot!!

OOPS! Sorry—who are you? Is it your party? Can we come?

QUARTZ!!!!!!!

No it isn't my birthday, but, yes, you can come to my party—it's a Welcome Home party my father is giving me. I don't deserve it, but Dad is pleased to see me.

Why? Where have you been?

It's a long story. I left home, with the money saved for when I was older. I had a brilliant time—lots of money, parties, friends... But soon the money ran out—no money, no parties, no friends, no food, no home...

No kidding!

I was desperate to go back home—even if it meant just being a servant.

And your dad is throwing a party for you? Wow!

For this son of mine was dead, but now he is alive, he was lost but now he has been found.

LUKE 15.24

This forgiveness thing has come up before hasn't it? Is it important in any friendship?

Yes! The other thing is to accept each other, even if we don't always get it right. I did some silly things, but I am still accepted.

What do you think the father and son are saying to each other?

Hold tight we're moving on!

Once again the Livewires looked around them.

We're back where we started. I recognize that place. What exactly is it?

It's a temple built by King Solomon. We thought you might like one last piece of wise advice on being good friends. Look, here comes Solomon now. You can ask him.

Now then, what can I do for you?

Ppp...ll...lease Sir, we're trying to find out how to be good friends. We've been having silly rows and we weren't speaking. It was horrible.

Tell me what you have learnt so far.

To keep on forgiving each other.

Not to gossip about one another.

To accept each other.

To be loyal to each other.

You have done very well. I will say one more thing.

Friends always show their love.

Thank you, dear Lord, for all the people who love me, especially...

Proverbs 17:17

The Livewires hugged each other to show that they loved each other. Boot and Tychi winked at each other and smiled.

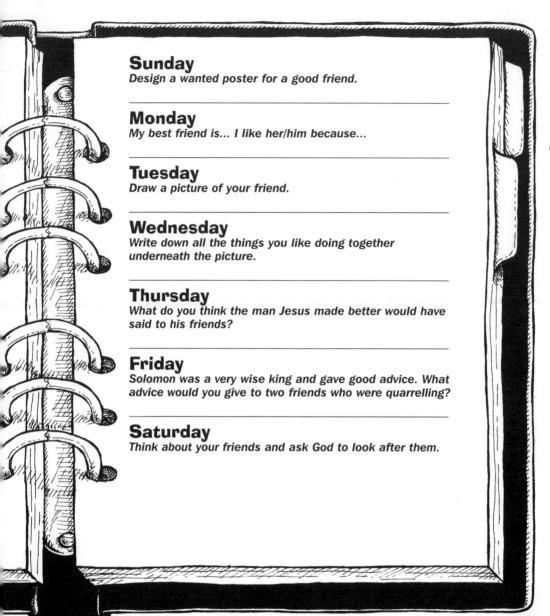

Sunday
Design a wanted poster for a good friend.

_____

Monday
My best friend is... I like her/him because...

_____

Tuesday
Draw a picture of your friend.

_____

Wednesday
Write down all the things you like doing together underneath the picture.

_____

Thursday
What do you think the man Jesus made better would have said to his friends?

_____

Friday
Solomon was a very wise king and gave good advice. What advice would you give to two friends who were quarrelling?

_____

Saturday
Think about your friends and ask God to look after them.

DIARY

The Livewires were so pleased to be friends again...

...everyone was shouting and cheering, but it was no good, they had lost again. They couldn't seem to get it together. They thought it would be easy to beat Boot and Tychi in a game of tug-of-war, but it didn't seem to be going very well. They started to blame each other for their lack of teamwork. They were pretty miserable.

I told you we should have had a plan.

And what sort of plan, may I ask?

This silly quarrelling went on for some time until Boot and Tychi looked at their long faces and decided it was time for action. Boot folded his arms and tapped his foot impatiently, would they never learn? There was a loud whirring noise and the Livewires found themselves right in the middle of a busy market.

Oh no! Where are we now? I wanted a quiet afternoon.

We're here in Jerusalem to find out how to work as a team.

The Livewires looked at each other. They moved closer together, afraid of being separated in the crowded market.

What's Jerusalem got to teach us about being a team?

The apostles went back to Jerusalem from the Mount of Olives, which is about a kilometre away from the city.

After Jesus was crucified, his closest friends were afraid, so they stuck together—an important part of team work. Stick together!

ACTS 1:12

Draw a cartoon picture of what you think it means to stick together.

Dear Lord, help me to stick with my friends, even when things aren't going well.

The Livewires suddenly caught sight of some people going into one of the houses which lined the market square.

Hey, look! Isn't that Simon Peter over there?

Boot smiled, nodded and gave a little bleep.

They gathered frequently to pray as a group, together with the women and with Mary the mother of Jesus and with his brothers.

ACTS 1:14

Where's Jesus then? Have I missed him?

Tychi gave a patient sigh.

This is after Jesus had gone back to be with his Father.

Gosh, it must have been strange without him around.

That's why it was important for his friends to be together and to pray together. Being together is an important part of being a team.

I get it! Being together and sticking together.

Draw a cartoon picture of what it means to 'be together'.

You're a fast learner, Little Ben!

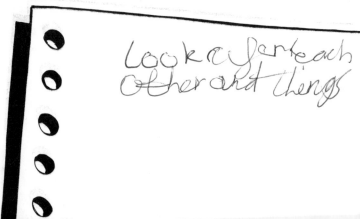

Look after each other and things

40

We spend a lot of time being together, and most of the time we stick together. So where did we go wrong with our tug-of-war?

Well, when we play football...

Not again!!!

... as I was saying, before each match we always plan our game. It helps us to know who is meant to do what—even if we don't always win.

Well, we certainly didn't plan anything. We just muddled through.

Tim's right. Planing together is an important part of being a team. When Jesus was no longer with them, his friends had to plan together. For example, they needed someone to take the place of Judas, who had betrayed Jesus.

Then they prayed, 'Lord, you know the thoughts of everyone, so show us which of these two you have chosen.'

I see, they didn't just talk about it, did they? They prayed about it and asked God to help them in their planning.

ACTS 1:24

While the Livewires were thinking about this, Tempo began running excitedly around them. He grabbed Data's rope which was lying on the ground and ran off into the market place. The Livewires charged after him, and ran straight into Peter.

Oops! Careful there! Hey, don't I know you from somewhere?

Hello, Peter! Yes, we're the Livewires—remember? We're trying to find out how a team works.

Well, you'd better come with me then and meet some of the team. Perhaps we can help you.

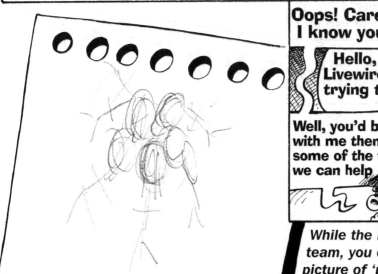

While the Livewires go and meet the team, you could draw your cartoon picture of 'planning together'.

The Livewires followed Peter to the house where they had seen him going in earlier with the others.

Are you having a party? I love parties! There's a lot of people here.

Day after day they met as a group in the Temple, and they had their meals together in their homes, eating with glad and humble hearts, praising God, and enjoying the good will of all the people.

ACTS 2:46

Peter laughed. 'No, it's not a party.' he said, 'We meet together every day, to eat, share and pray.

We all feel it's really important for us to meet together—it helps us to work more as a team. Sharing together is an important part of teamwork.

That's another thing we've learnt—sharing together. Sometimes we are selfish and don't share with each other. What were the other 'together' things a team should remember to do?

Can you remind Quartz what you have learnt so far? To help you remember, draw a cartoon picture of 'sharing together'.

Dear God, I'm sorry that sometimes I don't share with my friends.

Look after each other
sharing
planing —

It's not always easy. Some religious leaders don't like us telling people about Jesus, and they try to stop us. They even put us in prison.

Have you ever been in prison?

Oh, yes! John and I have both been in prison.

The Jewish leaders told us never to speak about Jesus again.

What did you say?

!

At that moment Boot jumped up and gave a bleep.

I think your funny square friend has something to say.

But Peter and John answered them, 'You yourselves judge which is right in God's sight—to obey you or to obey God.'

ACTS 4:19

That's what we said!

Did you both believe that?

Yes! We had to pull together against these leaders. We wanted them to see that they couldn't stop us.

Draw your cartoon picture of 'pulling together'.

If you hadn't pulled together your team would have been weaker.

You're right there, Little Ben.

We didn't pull together in our tug-of-war. We were all over the place!

One is easy break about is not

Philip went to tell the people of Samaria about Jesus, and lots of people believed, and many who were ill were made better.

It's good when you see the results of good teamwork. When we see people believing in Jesus it makes it all worthwhile.

So there was great joy in that city.

That's what I call winning together.

ACTS 8:8

Can you remember the 6 'together' things?

<u>sick</u> together   <u>sharing</u> together

<u>Pull</u> together   <u>winning</u> together

<u>Plan</u> together   <u>be</u> together

Can you think of any other 'together' things you need for working as a team?

20 FINISH	19	18 They all take Tempo for a walk. Move on 1 space.	17	16 No one will go to the disco with Quartz. Back 3 spaces.
11 Annie-log won't let others play with her new computer game. Back 3.	12	13	14 They all play a game with Little Ben. Move on 1 space.	15
10	9	8 The Livewires enjoy a day out together. Move on 3 spaces.	7	6 ? The Livewires forget to plan their game. Back 3 spaces.
1 START	2 Data is upset. Everyone looks after her. Move on 2 spaces..	3	4 Tim is cross no one will play football with him. Back 1 space.	5

The Livewires challenged some of Peter's team to a tug of war competition. While they are playing, perhaps you would like to play this game? Look at the diary on page 45 to see what to do.

Sunday

To play the game you need a dice and a counter for each person playing. Take turns to throw the dice and move your counter the number of spaces shown on the dice. Follow the instructions on the squares.

Monday

Make up your own game about teamwork. Ask a friend to play it with you.

Tuesday

Have you ever felt left out? What does it feel like? Remember you are never left out of God's love.

Wednesday

Draw a picture to show what 'winning together' means.

Thursday

How can you help someone at school who is often left out be part of a team?

Friday

Dear Father God, show me how to be part of your team.

Saturday

Draw a picture of the tug-of-war competition between the Livewires and Boot and Tychi. Who do you think will win this time?

whoaaa!!

The Livewires were feeling very confident about their teamwork and were talking about winning teams. Tim of course knew all the football teams, while Quartz knew who was top of the pops! They started discussing who they would most like to meet. Digit had written,

and was about to reveal the meaning when he fell against Boot, who bleeped loudly, and with a rush of air they were off again...

When everything had stopped spinning, the Livewires found Boot had landed them behind something very tall, very cold and very shiny. As they stood staring up at this amazing sight, which looked as if it were made of gold, they heard the sound of very loud music.

The Livewires cautiously peered around the side of the statue and stared at the amazing sight of hundreds of people on their knees—then they spotted three men still standing!!

The Livewires still do not know who Digit wanted to meet. Can you work it out?

Clue 1:   ⸬⊢ =e

As the Livewires stared at the crowd they saw the three men who were still standing, being taken away by guards.

Come on, let's see where they're being taken.

I'll slip my rope through Tempo's collar to stop him rushing off.

...ey slipped out *from* behind the statue and followed the guards. The three men were taken into a palace and the Livewires stood outside, not knowing what to do.

Those men are three friends of Daniel: Shadrach, Meshach and Abednego, and this is the king's palace.

Just at that moment they heard a loud voice shouting at the men.

Oh dear, the king doesn't sound too happy—all because they wouldn't bow down to the statue.

Gosh listen to that!! He's going to throw them into a blazing furnace if they don't bow down.

Fancy having to make that choice... Bow down or burn up, how awful!!

If the God whom we serve is able to save us from the blazing furnace and from your power, then he will. But even if he doesn't, Your Majesty may be sure that we will not worship your god, and we will not bow down to the gold statue that you have set up.

Amazing—they must really believe it's wrong to bow to the statue.

I'd like to meet someone who's brave enough to refuse a king, even if it means certain death. Wonder why it's wrong to bow to the statue?

DANIEL 3:17-18

Do you have any ideas what the answer to Tim's question might be?

Have you guessed who Digit wants to meet yet?

Clue 2:   ☉ = a

47

The Livewires were just wondering what would happen next when they heard a shout so loud they almost jumped out of their skins. Boot bleeped VERY loudly, Tempo ran for cover, dragging Data after him, and Tychi disappeared behind Boot.

What's happening, Boot?

Slowly Tychi reappeared and everyone looked at Boot

Then Nebuchadnezzar lost his temper, and his face turned red with anger at Shadrach, Meshach and Abednego. So he ordered his men to heat the furnace seven times hotter than usual.

DANIEL 3:19

Crumbs! He is more than angry.

Look they're coming out.

The Livewires hid behind a pillar. Shadrach, Meshach and Abednego were still saying they would not bow down to the statue because there was only one real God and they worshipped him.

Dear Lord, it's not always easy to be brave enough to stand up for you. Help us when we are asked to do something which isn't right to be brave enough to say no.

Tempo!!

Tempo had wriggled free from Data's grip and, dragging the rope behind him, rushed out from behind the pillar, barking loudly at the guards.

One of the guards made a grab for Tempo, but missed him and was left with just the rope in his hand.

The Livewires watched in horror as the guards used Data's rope to tie the men up.

Have you worked Digit's code out yet?
Clue 3: ☐ = h

The Livewires watched the guards as they took the men off to the furnace. They didn't know what to do. Tim and Digit wanted to follow the guards, but Annie-log wasn't so sure. They were wondering what to do next when suddenly they heard excited cries coming from the direction of the furnace. They could hear King Nebuchadnezzar shouting.

Suddenly Nebuchadnezzar leapt to his feet in amazement. He asked his officials, 'Didn't we tie up three men and throw them into the blazing furnace?' They answered, 'Yes, we did, Your Majesty.' 'Then why do I see four men walking in the fire?' he asked. 'They are not tied up, and they show no signs of being hurt—and the fourth one looks like a god.'

DANIEL 3:24 AND 25

They're not dead! They're alive and walking round. Amazing!

So God is looking after them. WOW!

I'm glad we stayed on to see the ending.

Now's the time for a party!

While the Livewires are celebrating you could draw Shadrach, Meshach and Abednego in the furnace with the angel God sent to look after them. Write what you think they might be saying to each other.

Dear Lord God, thank you for looking after Shadrach, Meshach and Abednego. Thank you for looking after me.

Clue 4: △ = n

People were gathering around the men to find out what had happened. There were so many that the Livewires could not see what was happening.

Their hair was not singed, their clothes were not burnt, and there was no smell of smoke on them.

Now that is something. I've only got to stand by the barbecue and I smell of smoke!

! !

DANIEL 3.27

King Nebuchadnezzar was very excited. He was jumping up and down and praising God.

Praise the God of Shadrach, Meshach, and Abednego! He sent his angel and rescued these men who serve and trust him. They disobeyed my orders and risked their lives rather than bow down and worship any god except their own.

Tim was so pleased he suggested a game of football to celebrate.

But the others wanted to sit quietly thinking about what had happened. They all felt that Shadrach, Meshach and Abednego had been very brave.

Think of a time when you had to be brave and say no to doing something you knew would be wrong to do. How did you feel about it?

Colour in the picture of King Nebuchadnezzar and the three brave men. Can you see where Data's rope is?

The King sent the following message to the people of all nations, races, and languages in the world: 'Greetings! Listen to my account of the wonders and miracles which the Supreme God has shown me. How great are the wonders God shows us! How powerful are the miracles he performs! God is king for ever; he will rule for all time.

DANIEL 4:1-3

Shadrach, Meshach and Abednego were thrilled that not only had God rescued them from the fiery furnace, but that King Nebuchadnezzar now believed in the one true God.

Come and join us! Let's fill the streets with singing and dancing!

We've met some interesting people. Who was it you wanted to meet Digit? Can you give us some clues?

You'll find her picture on stamps and bank notes!

I've got it—Queen Elizabeth!

Dear Lord God, help us to remember that others may be prepared to follow us if we are brave enough to do the right thing.

Sunday
Who would you most like to meet? Draw a picture of that person.

Monday
Write who your person is in code and see if someone can work out who it is.

Tuesday
Draw what you think the gold statue looked like.

Wednesday
Can you remember how big the statue was?

Thursday.
What would you have written in your diary that day if you had been Shadrach, Meshach or Abednego?

Friday
Think of some of the things you have done at school this week. Say a prayer for all those who work in your school—teachers, dinner ladies, cooks and any others who help.

Saturday
Is there someone you know who you could be extra friendly or helpful to?

Things were going well for the Livewires. They had enjoyed some wonderful adventures and had learnt some important lessons on friendship and teamwork. They were practising all they had learnt. Data's rope was proving very useful. They had used it for tug-of-war, high jump, skipping, goal posts and even as a lead for Tempo.

Not my idea of fun.

Boot was feeling hot and bothered after yet another game of tug-of-war. He thought back to how he had worked at teaching the Livewires to be a team... Wouldn't it be good to paddle his feet in the sea... suddenly he began to whirr and bleep.

Here we go again...!

The Livewires came to rest with a bump. They were looking out at the Sea of Galilee, sitting next to three men. It was very peaceful—no one wanted to break the silence.

Look who it is... Hi kids, hi Boot. Sorry ... Hi Tychi.

Do we know you? You look sort of familiar.

We're a bit older than when we last met. I'm Andrew, this is James and John. Remember?

Looking back and remembering.

Of course. What are you doing here?

Tychi typed something into Boot and they all looked.

He went on and saw two other brothers, James and John, the sons of Zebedee... getting their nets ready. Jesus called them, and at once they left the boat and their father, and went with him.

MATTHEW 4:21–22

Yes, that's how it all started. That's a good day to remember—Jesus coming and calling us to be his disciples.

While the Livewires are being reminded of that day you could write down all the good memories you have. Perhaps you could write a prayer in the prayer cloud thanking God for all those good times?

Andrew, James and John did not need any encouragement to talk about the things that had happened to them over the years.

Do you remember this?

They all looked at Boot's screen.

'There is a boy here who has five loaves of barley bread and two fish. But they will certainly not be enough for all these people.'

Of course I remember... I didn't know what was going to happen but I knew I had to take the boy to Jesus.

JOHN 6:9

We're glad he did. Everyone was pretty hungry, including us. There were about 5,000 altogether. Jesus said we had to feed the people, but we had no idea how. No money— no food.

So what happened?

Jesus prayed and gave out the bread and fish. Believe it or not there was enough for everyone to eat and there were twelve baskets of pieces left over.

Once again Jesus surprised us.

I bet that little boy remembers the time he helped Jesus.

Imagine you are the little boy who gave the loaves and fishes to Jesus. Write a letter to your friend telling him/her what happened.

Dear...

I remember going to Wembley to watch the Cup Final. It was mega brilliant.

I remember going to a pop concert. It was fantastic.

I remember when my mum took Annie-log and me to the cinema as a treat because we had both been ill in bed.

I remember a nice juicy bone... mmmm.

Simon's mother-in-law was sick in bed with a fever, and as soon as Jesus arrived, he was told about her.

I'd forgotten about that. Do you two remember?

It seems ages ago, but I remember what happened.

MARK
1:30

If you know someone who is not well, say a prayer for that person.

Tell us. Was it good or bad?

Definitely good. We went to our house with Jesus and when he heard about Simon's mother-in-law, he made her better. She was so well she made a meal for us. We were all thrilled.

It's good to remember isn't it?

Dear Lord, I'm thinking about... who's not well. Please be with them, and help them to get better soon.

Soon the Livewires were talking about things they didn't want to remember.

I once wiped a whole lot of Dad's work from his computer because I thought I knew how to work it properly. He was not pleased with me.

I got stuck down a rabbit hole once— Embarrassing!

Some time ago I was so mean to a girl at school that I made her cry. I felt awful about it and I cried. We made up afterwards.

Did you guys ever do or say anything you wished you hadn't?

James and John looked at each other and didn't know what to say, when Boot bleeped. They looked at the screen.

Oh no, not that time!

I'd rather forget that. I feel embarrassed to think about it.

They asked Jesus, 'When you sit on your throne in your glorious Kingdom, we want you to let us sit with you, one at your right and one at your left.'

What's wrong with that?

MARK 10:37

Well, we wanted to be more important than all the other disciples. When they found out what we had been asking they were cross with us.

Jesus told us we all had to serve each other and not try to be the most important.

We learnt our lesson—and we realized something else which is very important...

Yes, we know that God understands when we do and say the wrong things. He forgives us and helps us not to do it again.

Have you had any embarrassing moments? Or have you said things you wished you hadn't?

Help Tempo choose the right path to get himself out of the rabbit hole.

56

The Livewires noticed that James and John had gone very quiet. They looked thoughtful, and a bit upset.

You look as if you are thinking about something sad.

Then he came back to his disciples and found them asleep; they could not keep their eyes open. And they did not know what to say to him.

Was that you two?

MARK 14:40

James and John nodded quietly and told them what had happened.

Just before Jesus was arrested we all went with him to the Garden of Gethsemane. Then he took us and Peter a little further on and asked us to keep watch while he prayed. Each time he returned we had fallen asleep.

It's awful to think how badly we let Jesus down at such an important time.

It's sad when we let others down. Remember how we learnt earlier that if we say sorry we can be forgiven?

All was still and silent as they thought of people they had let down, and said their own sorry prayers.

Perhaps you would like to say your own sorry prayers? You could write them on a piece of paper.

Then tear up the piece of paper and throw it away.

God forgives us and helps us not to do it again.

The Livewires were enjoying sharing memories, even if some of them were sad memories.

Have you remembered anything else you can tell us before we have to move on?

What a lovely memory that is.

Then Jesus came and stood among them. 'Peace be with you,' he said.

JOHN 20:19

That happened a few days after Jesus had been crucified and his body had gone from the tomb. We were all afraid of the Jewish authorities, so we hid away together behind locked doors.

While we were together, Jesus suddenly appeared and gave us his peace. We were so happy—we thought he was dead, but he was alive. He knew we were afraid and he gave us his peace.

PEACE BE WITH YOU

The Livewires thought that was a lovely thing to remember—Jesus bringing peace to the disciples who were afraid.

Perhaps you could design a card with the words 'Peace be with you' on it. You could give it to someone who is special to you.

Sunday
Did you think of many nice memories? Draw a picture of one of them.

Monday
Design your own 'Thank You' card to someone special.

Tuesday
How many people did Jesus feed with the boy's loaves and fishes?

Wednesday

Dear Lord, thank you for all my friends, and all the people who help me. Help me to remember to say 'thank you' to them.

Thursday
Can you remember what Jesus told James and John when they tried to be more important than the others? What does it mean to 'serve' others?

Friday
Write down the feelings that you would connect with peace.

Saturday
Remember in the coming week that God is with you and can give you his peace.

Ooops!

The Livewires began to feel sleepy sitting on the beach with Andrew, James and John. Tempo dozed right off. He must have been dreaming of rabbits because he wagged his tail in his sleep, hitting Boot's keyboard. Boot began to whirr and everything began to go hazy. Suddenly they found themselves sitting in another peaceful place, but indoors this time...

WHiiRRRRRR

It was very quiet and peaceful and as the Livewires looked around they realized Boot had brought them to a rather beautiful church. The sun shone through the stained glass windows, throwing rays of light onto the floor and the large table at the front of the church. Little Ben rubbed his eyes, amazed at the wonderful patterns it made. They all felt peaceful and nobody wanted to talk or break the silence.

As they looked around they saw a cross, a candle, a picture of a dove and many other things. Data liked the picture of the dove in the stained glass window and asked why it was there.

Boot bleeped quietly.

As soon as Jesus was baptized, he came up out of the water. Then heaven was opened to him, and he saw the Spirit of God coming down like a dove and alighting on him. Then a voice said from heaven, 'This is my own dear Son, with whom I am pleased.'

MATTHEW 3:16-17

The dove reminds us of the Holy Spirit which God gives to all his people. We don't always remember that God is with us so it is good to have something like the dove to remind us. It's a bit like having photographs of friends so that we don't forget them.

The Livewires started thinking about things they had collected to remind them of special times. Annie-log had kept her very first computer game, Tim had the programme from the first football match he had gone to and Data still had all her birthday cards.

Clues
1. Tim saved this
2. You keep them in an album
3. Sent through the post—people often collect these
4. Tempo collects these!
5. You get this for coming first
6. Something hard to throw away!
7. Data collects these

Can you think of any things you have kept to remind you of something special?

What special things can you find hidden in this wordsearch?

```
p r o g r a m m e
h s t b o n e s o
o p q c a r d s n
t o y s t a a m p
o n e u o b l e e
s t a m p s i t o
```

The Livewires wandered around the church looking with interest at so many different things. Suddenly the peace was shattered when they heard Tim shouting that he had found a bird bath in the church!! They ran to look. Boot bleeped and Tychi sighed. The Livewires couldn't stop laughing! Tim didn't know what the joke was.

Oh, Tim! That's not a bird bath! It's a font!

A font is where you put the water to baptize someone, which is then sprinkled over their head.

In some churches they have something like a large pool and people are baptized by going completely under the water. I remember being told about that at Sunday School.

It is through faith that all of you are God's children in union with Christ Jesus. You were baptized into union with Christ.

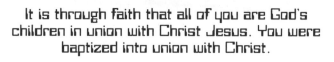

When we are baptized the water is a sign of God washing all the bad things from inside us and welcoming us into his family.

GALATIANS 3:26-27

I always need a bath after football!

So, when we are dirty on the outside, we wash to make ourselves clean...

...and when we are dirty on the inside, God washes us to make us clean?

That's right, Data!

Father God, thank you that...

Have you ever been to a baptism? You could draw a picture of the person being baptized being welcomed into God's family. Write their name in the prayer cloud.

is a member of your family. Amen.

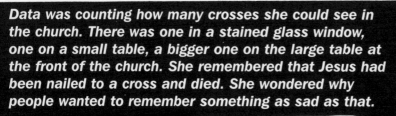

Data was counting how many crosses she could see in the church. There was one in a stained glass window, one on a small table, a bigger one on the large table at the front of the church. She remembered that Jesus had been nailed to a cross and died. She wondered why people wanted to remember something as sad as that.

Thank you Jesus for dying for me

We have the cross as a reminder that Jesus died on the cross so that we can be forgiven and can know God for ourselves.

For by the death of Christ we are set free, that is, our sins are forgiven.

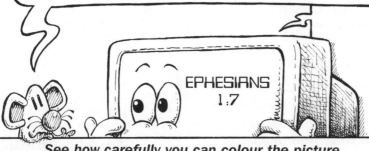

EPHESIANS 1:7

See how carefully you can colour the picture.

'I am the light of the world,' Jesus said. 'Whoever follows me will have the light of life and will never walk in darkness.'

JOHN 8:12

The Livewires looked around the church to see if there was anything that would help them remember that Jesus was the light of the world.

Perhaps it's the stained glass?

Perhaps it's that big Bible?

After a while Quartz shouted...

I've got it—a candle!

She was right. Boot looked pleased and stood under the tall candle which was burning softly on the table at the front of the church. It's light shone on his screen.

I remember a time when there was a power cut at home, Mum and Dad lit candles. I was surprised how much light they gave.

We often light candles in church to help us to remember Jesus is the light of the world. They remind us that Jesus is with us even in hardest times, when everything seems dark and horrible.

Yes, we were really glad we had them.

RTWAE
EDOV
SCRSO
LDNCAE

Digit was busy doodling on his pad. He has mixed up the letters for the four different Christian symbols the Livewires have been finding out about. Can you sort them out? You may like to draw a picture of each of them.

Annie-log started typing the words into Boot. Suddenly she pressed ESCape by mistake... the church seemed to swirl around before their eyes as Boot began to whirr.

Tim only just had time to grab hold of Tempo who was looking for mice under the pews. Quartz grasped hold of Data, with Tychi swinging on the rope which was sticking out of her pocket.

Annie-log!!! You might have warned us!!!

... and they landed with a bump... back in Annie-log's bedroom. Boot gave a small bleep and went very quiet. There was just the hint of candle wax on his screen...